Psychology and Crime

Thomas Holmes

Psychology and Crime

The present edition is a reproduction of previous publication of this classic work. Minor typographical errors may have been corrected without note; however, for an authentic reading experience the spelling, punctuation, and capitalization have been retained from the original text.

ISBN: 979-8-88830-356-6

CONTENTS

PREFACE

Sincerely do I hope that the issue of this little book may prove useful in drawing the attention of the public to the mental and physical condition of the unfortunates who form such a large proportion of our prison population.

To our authorities the sad plight of this mass of smitten humanity is well known. Year after year our Prison Commissioners, in presenting their reports, have not failed to impress upon the State the great part physical and mental afflictions play in the production of crime.

So far, the information given by the Prison Commissioners has produced little or no effect; neither have their representations led to any alteration in the treatment of unfortunate individuals whose infirmities are in reality the root cause of their delinquency.

To the official information I add the result of my own prolonged experience. This experience has imbued me with the conviction that the present methods of dealing with suffering humanity are neither wise, just, nor efficacious. I have seen the helplessness of so many that are called criminals that, in writing these pages, I am animated with a keen desire to hasten the day of sensible reform. Surely the day cannot be far distant when the State will take mental and physical infirmities into consideration when it has to deal with its erring children.

Thomas Holmes
Howard Association,
Devonshire Chambers, Bishopsgate.

CHAPTER I

PSYCHOLOGY AND CRIME

I hope that no one will be prevented from reading this chapter by its title, for let me say at once that I am not the least bit scientific. Whatever I have to say will be expressed in very simple language, and further, that in the writing of it I am animated with the desire of conveying to thoughtful and non-scientific readers some of the personal causes that lead individuals to commit actions that are deemed criminal.

Of the social and industrial causes of crime I shall be silent, for whole volumes have been and can still be written on those subjects, and though to me they are very inviting topics, I must within the compass of this little book ignore them.

I shall of course speak "right on" and tell of what I have seen and known during my many years' experience of London's criminals.

Indeed, I have no other qualification than this: that for twenty-five years I have spent my days in London police courts, and my evenings with discharged prisoners.

I may also add to these opportunities for study, frequent visits to prisons, and confidential talks with prisoners.

It will, I think, be admitted that I have had privileged opportunities for learning something, but by no means everything, of the characteristics, mentality and personality of law-breakers.

Of a certainty, considering the extent of my opportunities, I must have been dull if I had not learned much, or what is perhaps of more importance, unlearned a great deal more about the personal causes of crime.

I will therefore draw upon my own experience, feeling quite sure that a non-scientific book, though small in size and free from pretensions, will be a welcome addition to the long list of books that have been written upon this interesting subject.

To me it is a most inviting subject, yet it is a singularly dangerous one; for when any one undertakes to explain the working of another man's mind, and to give reasons for the other man's actions, he assumes a knowledge that he cannot possess, though he may honestly believe that he possesses it. In reality he makes statements that cannot be proved, but they are statements that cannot be disproved.

The list of scientific books on this subject is a long one, indeed it is almost interminable. Many of these books are voluminous in size and terrifying in title. Some of these, written by men of eminence, have their uses, and may be considered standard works. Neither can there be the slightest doubt that the accumulated experience, research or opinions of thinking men have, and have very rightly, a title to serious consideration.

But when any book professes to be a kind of mental "ready reckoner" for judges, magistrates and others who are called upon to adjudicate upon the guilt or innocence of individuals, and to apportion punishment, I for one feel suspicious as to the value of that book for its specified purpose.

It is, no doubt, a comforting thought to many who have to sit in judgment upon others, that they can have access to books written by learned scientists that will afford them light and leading on the mysteries of criminal psychology.

But is it possible to explore the innermost recesses of a criminal's mind, or to follow the workings of passion, instinct, mania or whim in any selected prisoner?

With all respect I venture to say it is not possible. The pretension to such knowledge is at once dangerous and misleading; and though many things in a book of this description may be true and instructive, the great bulk of it must be pure conjecture. So far as my experience goes, no two criminals are alike; but while they vary as ordinary people vary, they are far more careful than ordinary people to conceal their thoughts, and, believe me, they are far more successful in their endeavours.

As a matter of fact, the criminal, especially the habitual criminal, lives in a world of self-repression. In prison he is not only shut up, but he also shuts himself up. He gives nothing away to his would-be investigators.

He is cute enough to know what the investigator is after, and clever enough to give answers that will please his questioner and confirm him in judgments that he has already formed: though probably there is not more than a grain of truth in the whole of the answers he will give. I am led to these remarks by the fact that all round me as I write are books that deal with the crime of the world, hundreds of them, and a weird collection they form.

As I sit and look at them they fascinate me, almost cast a spell over me. But when I rise from my desk, take one into my hand and read but a single page, I am disillusioned.

For I realise that the writer knows no more of the true inwardness of things appertaining to the criminal mind, than ordinary observant men may know.

True, he can mystify us with scientific terms; he can talk about the conscious and the subconscious, and many other speculative things. He can give us measurements of the body and describe the exact angle at which a criminal's ears stand, and the angle at which his chin recedes.

But when from these he proceeds to reveal the recesses of the mind at the back of the big ears, or the little chins, we feel that we are on an equality with the writer, for we know as much upon the matter as scientists or specialists can know.

Now these books have been written by all sorts of people: doctors of law and of medicine, scientists, professors, governors and chaplains of prisons, journalists and self-appointed specialists.

Mostly they come to us from the continent of Europe, where the various schools of psychological thought contend for mastery.

The Lombrosian school tells us how to detect the criminal by his physical conformation, or by the convolutions of his brain; but as the brain cannot be dissected while the criminal lives, this method of identification is of no practical use.

Another school will tell us how to detect the criminal by his behaviour whilst undergoing interrogation or standing his trial, when, not only his appearance, but his actions also are to be closely observed by judge and jury.

Should the accused smooth the hair upon his head with his hand, it is a sign of fear, for he feels a sensation at the roots of his hair as though each particular hair was standing on its end. He therefore involuntarily attempts to smooth it down. Now all this may be true, but it conveys nothing, and to take it as a sign of guilt is childishly absurd.

A perfectly innocent person may have a greater sense of fear than the most guilty criminal, for certainly the ultimate consequences of the trial are to him of far greater importance, and more likely to produce the sensation of fear. I have before me the latest addition to this class of book, so far as England is concerned. It numbers no less than five hundred pages, and each page contains at least four hundred words.

It comes to us from Austria, via America. Its translation into English must have been a stupendous task, for the author has laid the world under contribution, and given us selections from, and references to, hundreds of books dealing with criminal psychology: the result being an intensely interesting book.

Just how far the demeanour, actions and traits of foreign criminals may furnish safe guidance in the judgment of English prisoners, neither author nor translator tell us. But as the peculiarities of crime and criminals are generally questions of latitude and longitude, climate, environment, social condition and national temperament, so it seems to me that the psychology and mannerism of criminals must differ accordingly, and that the rules set up for guidance in one part of the world may be quite inapplicable to another part.

The author tells us that this book is a "manual" for judges, practitioners and students; for it deals not only with the psychology of criminals or suspected criminals, but with that of judges, magistrates, witnesses and police also. To every thoughtful layman I would heartily recommend this book, for it is well worth reading and pondering; but I would rigidly prevent all judges, magistrates and jurymen having access to it. Why? Because it is their business and prerogative to decide upon the guilt or innocence of the prisoner according to the weight of the evidence, every detail of which demands their concentrated attention if justice is to be done.

I can imagine nothing more disastrous to the administration of justice than a course of study of what is called criminal psychology. Students of human nature I would have them all to be, for such study is essential and leads to nothing but good. But to issue "manuals" that profess to instruct them upon the mysterious working of the human mind; to teach them to weigh the relative worth of provincial mannerism and individual characteristics; to tell the value of a look of the eyes, the smile of the face, and the movement of the hands; to teach them to notice all these things, and then by a process of inductive reasoning to decide upon the guilt or innocence of the individual may be criminal psychology, but it is rubbish none the less, and dangerous rubbish too!

Do the eminent writers of these books ever consider the effect likely to be produced on the minds of judges, magistrates and jurors who may read, believe and adopt their teaching?

Humbly, but very earnestly, I say that any magistrate, judge or juror who is steeped in this kind of teaching is quite unfitted by his supposed knowledge for the task he has in hand. For of all men, judges require the open mind and the clean slate and with them there must be no judgment formed apart from the evidence of fact. They of all men must not be inflated with the idea that they can "read people"—can see through them; that they, independently of evidence, can give a correct judgment.

Let us suppose that we compelled our magistrates, great and small, to pass an examination in criminal psychology, using these "manuals" as textbooks. I venture to say that a queer state of things would follow. The action of magistrates would be dominated by their own individual psychology, and their own psychology would be dominated by the effect the "manual" had produced on their mind. The shallow man would be assured of his competence and knowledge, and he would, to his own satisfaction at least, know all about it. But the greater man would hesitate; he would be in a quandary, on the horns of a dilemma, for he would find that the formula of his "manual," by which he was to form an opinion as to the guilt of the prisoner, applied with equal force to the innocence of the prisoner.

Let us suppose a case where three magistrates form a Bench, each having been trained according to the "manual." No. 1 is certain; No. 2 is diffident, and No. 3 is a dreamer and greatly interested in subconsciousness.

A prisoner is before them on a disgraceful charge; he is innocent, and has hitherto lived an irreproachable life. The prisoner protests his innocence, but cannot control himself; he wipes his brow, he smooths his hair, he clenches his fist, and his eyes flash fiercely.

Magistrate No. 1 notices all these things and says to himself: "The prisoner has no self-control; he is in fear, he is passionate, he is charged with a crime of passion, he is guilty!" But magistrate No. 2 also notices all these things and says to himself: "The prisoner is indignant, he feels his position acutely, for he is a respectable man; he fears the consequences the more because he is an innocent man; I am for his acquittal, but I am not sure, for his bearing is compatible with guilt or innocence." Magistrate No. 3 has been eagerly looking for some proof of subconsciousness, and not having discovered any, he is uninterested in the mental equation that excites his colleagues.

Happy will that Bench be if it possesses a common-sensed old chairman who has not graduated in criminal psychology: who is content to be guided entirely by the actual evidence; and happy will it be for the innocent prisoner too!

So far as I have read these "manuals," and so far as my personal experience goes—and it is not a short one—I have discovered no outward and visible signs that indicate a prisoner's guilt that may not at the same time be taken as an indication of the prisoner's innocence.

But supposing that our worthy magistrates, not being satisfied on psychological grounds, or for other reasons, decide to commit the prisoner for trial by judge and jury. Why, then, there will be curious happenings if judge and jury, with prosecuting and defending counsel, have been trained as per "manual."

For the psychology of the various witnesses must be examined, declared and rebutted. The mentality of the police must be exposed, dilated upon, attacked and defended, and a clever lawyer would find ample scope for his ability by probing and peering into the mind of his lordship the judge. Really there would be no end to the possibilities, and a pretty state of things would eventuate, for the jury, although having previously given satisfactory proof that their minds were in good working order, would before the end be reduced to a psychological state bordering on imbecility, and would be rendered quite incapable of any but a confused judgment.

No, I am not exaggerating, for one "manual" in my possession gives instruction upon all these and hundreds of other useless points.

This may be considered as psychology run mad; nevertheless, it is a state of things that is likely to come about if we are guided by scientists, and the present trend is certainly in this direction.

Let me, therefore, before it is too late, register a protest against the assumption that it is necessary for our judges and magistrates to be trained in what is not and can never be an exact science: criminal psychology.

But let them be trained to weigh and assort actual evidence, for this has hitherto been the glory of the English jurists. Institute we well may some training for justices of the peace, and it would be well if they were submitted to some examination that their capabilities for the work might be tested; but to put books into their hands which profess to explain the workings of a prisoner's mind, and to reveal his hidden thoughts, is a plan at once futile and dangerous.

While I am persuaded that it will be well for us if our judges, magistrates and jurors are not requested to take honours in psychology, I am still more firmly convinced that it will be a bad day for us when science or evolution provides us with mental rays that will enable us to explore the criminal mind. I would allow even the worst of men to have something of his own, sacred to himself—some corner, even though it be a dark one, into which he can retire with the certainty that no one can follow him.

Punish him if we must! pity him we certainly should! control and reform him if we can! But let us make no attempt to turn him inside out and exhibit his mental organisation to curious people by a series of mental photography.

For should that day come, it will be an evil one for some respectable people, for the rays will be turned upon us, and not to our comfort! Some very good people that I know will turn out disappointments, and our faith in each other will vanish.

For one reason, and one reason only, I would like such rays to exist: they would show us that there is little difference between the criminal and the ordinary law-abiding citizen; and in reckoning the sum total of good and evil in each I am not certain that the criminal would always come off the worst.

But I am sure that we shall be in for lively times when we are able to explore each other's minds.

There is that fellow Brown, he is a mystery to me; I feel sure that he is a rascal; I can't imagine how he gets a living. He is a dangerous man! I avail myself of the first opportunity and turn my rays upon him; I rake him fore and aft, nothing escapes me, horrified though I am; I find him worse than I expected, but I take my mental photograph and use it too! I think it my duty to warn my friends against him. Brown hears of it and meets me — result: physical, not psychological, reasons keep me at home for a week.

Would the world be happier, would justice be better administered if we acquired through science "manuals" or evolution powers of this description? I think not! Better, I say, a hundred times better for us to remain in our present state of ignorance, thinking the best of each other, than for us to "probe in the bowels of unwelcome truth."

But the study of criminal psychology has its place, or ought to have its place, and an important place too, in our penal administration; and our prisons, when they are properly conducted, will become at once mental and physical observatories.

It is in this department of administration, not in courts of justice, the criminal psychologist may pursue his investigations, exercise his powers and develop his science without fear of doing any serious wrong. Not that prison is of all places the best, but for the reason that in prison material is always at hand for the purpose. But I shall deal with this more fully in another chapter.

CHAPTER II

PHYSIOLOGY AND CRIME

In this chapter I want to show that crime generally does not proceed from sheer wickedness, or the desire to be criminal. I am anxious to burn this into the brain and conscience of the nation. I would like our authorities to accept it as an axiom! For then they would seek as far as possible to understand our criminals, and getting knowledge of them, they would deal differently with them. And dealing differently with them would bring blessed results, for many of our prisons would become useless; they would be untenanted!

I maintain that the most serious causes of crime are physiological, not psychological. And though in all probability we shall remain impotent with regard to psychological causes, there is not the slightest reason why we should not learn a great deal more about, and do a great deal to cure or prevent, the physiological causes of crime. Perhaps if I were a scientist I would say pathological causes, but I use the word "physiological" to denote all bodily conditions other than brain disease. This, too, is of course physical, though we term it mental, for the brain is matter as truly as it is mind. I am ashamed to confess that I do not know where the physical ends and the mental begins, neither can I tell at what point the pathological ends and the psychological begins, for psychology is but extended physiology.

The body acts upon the mind, and the mind upon the body in so many, and in such mysterious ways, that I cannot differentiate between them. But of one thing I am quite certain, and it is this: that the best way to learn something of a criminal's mind is to ascertain everything possible with regard to his body.

In prison this can easily be done, for in prison there is an abundance of time, ample opportunity, and a sufficiency of means for this interesting study. In one Continental prison this is done. There the doctor, not the governor, is the most important personage. From him I sometimes get very instructive communications. The author of the "manual" quoted tells us "that it is his aim to present such a psychology as will deal with all states of mind that might possibly be involved in the determination and judgment of crime." This is a large order, for he promises an impossibility. I marvel at his temerity, I am then struck by his audacity. But on consulting his index and searching his five hundred pages I admire his prudence, for he never attempts to keep his promise. I find no reference to the influence that physical disease, affliction or deprivation exercises upon the mind. Of epileptics he has nothing to say. He ignores afflictions!

Of the blind, the deaf and dumb he is apparently unaware; the cripple, the hunchback, the maimed, the one-armed, the one-legged, the sufferers from sunstroke, and the vast army whose lives have been spoiled through physical accidents—of their psychology we are told nothing.

Yet every one knows, or might know, that their psychological condition is absolutely dominated by their physical condition. In each of them physical nature has been outraged, it has been assaulted; and Nature, knowing no pity, hits back again with a vengeance.

We know, or we might if we cared to know, that these unfortunates, having suffered loss, must receive compensation of some kind, and if that compensation be not of a comforting and inspiring character, including training, education, control and new favourable developments, they become potential criminals. Their wits become sharpened to deceive, their tempers violent, explosive and dangerous. Some one has said, "I am my body." While this may not be wholly true, there is still a world of truth in the statement. So I again suggest that before we try to grope in the dark recesses of the mind, we set to work to learn more of the body, for that is an open book.

Believe me, it is given to very few to bear about with them a deformed, mutilated or afflicted body without their minds becoming changed also.

Verily, the writers of our old fairy tales and our early novelists were not very far wrong. Have any of my readers ever walked through Parkhurst prison? It is a sort of convalescent home for criminals—a sanatorium, if you will, in the Isle of Wight.

If you have not, then come with me in imagination! Never mind the building, take no heed of the officials, let us concentrate our attention on the prisoners, the criminals, for they are all undergoing penal servitude.

You gasp! and well you may. You never saw such a strange, pitiful mass of smitten humanity! Well! that is something to be thankful for.

"Do you want any specialist in psychology to reveal the working of their queer minds?" "No," you say, "their poor bodies reveal their minds." "But they are convicts." "Oh, no," you say, "surely they are patients."

And patients they ought to be; but convicts the law declares them, and convicts they will remain till their smitten bodies and poor minds part company.

I declare that this criminal psychology business makes me hot! It is criminal physiology we should be after, not psychology.

But let us go back to Parkhurst, and talk the matter over.

In Parkhurst there is a daily average of over 750 convicts, of whom nearly one-fourth are under hospital treatment.

The death-rate is high in spite of great medical care and healthy environment, and in spite of the number of prisoners released on account of their health.

The number of consumptives in 1909 was 34, of whom 14 were new admissions and 13 others were noted as having disease of the lungs previous to their reception; 3 prisoners died of this disease during the year. But hear this—for I am quoting from an official report for 1909-10.

"The number classified as weak-minded at the end of the year was 117, but in addition 34 other convicts were attached to parties of weak-minded for further mental observation."

Now, add together the hospital patients, the consumptives, the weak-minded and those suspected of mental weakness, subtract them from the total 750 convicts; how many have we left? I don't know, I have no means of knowing. But we will suppose that one-half of them are neither invalids nor weak-minded. March them out! let us look at them; one look is enough, what have we seen? Blighted bodies! twisted bodies! and mutilated bodies! retarded physical growth accompanied with undeveloped minds. Bleared eyes and defective eyesight, epileptics and similar sufferers, a motley, pitiful assemblage of unfortunate humanity, and alas! hopeless humanity.

You say, "But these broken fellows cannot commit crime." Can't they? here is a list of their crimes tabulated by the medical officer for State purposes, but it refers to the weak-minded only: False pretences 3; receiving stolen property 3; larceny 18; burglary 7; house- or shop-breaking 19; uttering counterfeit coin 1; threatening letters 4; threatening violence 1; robbery with violence 3; manslaughter 6; wounding with intent 8; grievous bodily harm 2; attempted murder 1; wilful murder 7; rape 5;

arson 15; carnal knowledge of little girls 8; cattle-maiming 1; placing obstruction on railway 2; unnatural offence 3; total 117.

"An awful list," you say. "Yes, but it is an illuminating list!" Again I quote: "During the year 35 convicts were certified as insane and sent to asylums"; work that out in your minds, think of it! "Why," you say, "the State has been punishing them when they are not responsible; it has been tabulating them as criminals when it ought to have restrained them as patients!" True! for the State awarded an average of something like seven years' penal servitude to each of them for their last sentence only. Now, what reasonable man wants to know more about the psychology of these men than is apparent to any one who possesses eyes and can use them?

But let us listen to the chaplain, and here I quote from his official report—

"The large number of 'weak-minded' cases located here adds considerably to the strain imposed by prison work.

"Many of them are irritable and very exacting in their demands for individual attention.

"We do our best to meet their requirements, and find that patience and kindness go a long way in allaying their excitement. The work amongst this class of prisoner is highly interesting, but I sincerely regret that their prospects on discharge are no brighter.

"In many cases freedom simply means a relapse into crime, from sheer inability to obtain or follow any ordinary occupation.

"It is surely time that some comprehensive scheme be started for dealing with these unfortunate creatures.

"It is worthy of note that out of the 142 weak-minded prisoners confined here in 1908-9, only 8 could be held responsible for their lamentable state, their weak-minded condition being attributed to over-indulgence in alcohol. 'Unfortunate' seems, therefore, a correct description of this class of prisoner, who are really more deserving of pity than punishment, and certainly call for special treatment on discharge.

"There are a considerable number of senile and debilitated convicts here, many of whom have several convictions recorded against them. They are absolutely unfitted for employment, and on release have to face one of two alternatives—the workhouse or another period of imprisonment. The great majority openly confess their preference for a penal establishment, and I am convinced that a large number deliberately commit a crime which will ensure their return to this prison.

"The State would save a considerable sum annually if such men could be placed, under a medical certificate, on an old age pension list, or boarded out in some home under proper supervision. It would be interesting to watch an experiment tried with a few selected cases of senile prisoners released on a conditional licence.

"This is a somewhat revolutionary suggestion, perhaps; but the problem of dealing with habitual offenders who are incapable of work is worthy of consideration, and needs solution."

But I may be told that Parkhurst is an exceptional prison, and that it is intended chiefly for weaklings.

This is quite true, but it is beside the question; for the inhabitants of Parkhurst are convicts, men who have, as my list shows, committed serious crime; that they have been gathered from other prisoners goes to prove my point, viz., that physical causes which are evident demand attention to an infinitely greater degree than speculative and obscure causes that we cannot diagnose, and which, for all we know, may not exist.

But what obtains at Parkhurst exists in every other prison, unless it be a specialised prison such as Borstal in England, and Elmira in America.

Year after year in their annual report the Prison Commissioners tell us, and they are never tired of telling us, that our prisons are filled with the very poor, the very weak, the afflicted and the ignorant.

I could fill a volume with extracts from reports with such testimony; governors, chaplains and medical officers with wearying monotony have testified to the same effect.

Has not their accumulated evidence been published in Blue books? It has; but it has suffered the fate to which all Blue books are doomed, for it has been buried with the dead past. The Prison Commissioners have taken infinite pains to ascertain the truth, and have not been slow in declaring the truth so far as it has been revealed to them.

They tell us that for ten years they have in Pentonville prison measured, weighed and medically examined all the young prisoners, i.e., all those under twenty-one years of age who have undergone sentences in that huge establishment.

Many thousands of such prisoners have passed through Pentonville during those ten years, and a terrible procession of smitten humanity they have presented.

Listen, my lords and gentlemen of both Houses! Heed! all Social Reformers of every kind! Think of it, all you specialists who claim to explore the criminal mind! "On an average they are two inches less in height, and fourteen pounds less in weight than the average industrial population of similar ages; 28 per cent. of them suffer from some physical disease or deprivation," and then the report goes on to add "the highest proportion of reconvictions was amongst this class, being no less than 40 per cent."

I demand attention to this statement; nay, it demands and should compel attention of itself.

This very bald statement of a stupendous fact ought to make us think.

Thousands, tens of thousands of young fellows, two inches below their proper height, fourteen pounds less than their proper weight, twenty-eight out of every hundred physically afflicted, and forty out of every hundred reconvicted again and again!!

Who cares to trouble about their psychology? Not I! But I do care and want others to care a great deal about their bodies, so I say let psychology go hang! Let us concentrate on their bodies.

And my own observation, in prison and outside prison, confirms these startling facts.

Hundreds of young fellows who have served short sentences of imprisonment find their way to my house or to my office. I rarely find a full-sized and well-developed fellow amongst them, for, mostly, they are of the class described by the Prison Commissioners.

Round shoulders, flat chests and flat feet, poor teeth, sore eyes, are ever noticeable, while not a few point me to their maimed hands or other limbs and tell me of their illnesses.

I am heartily tired of meeting with such afflicted humanity that I cannot help or assist in any useful way.

But I want no specialist or professor to read me their minds, for their bodies are their minds.

These young fellows are not particularly wicked; they have no great passion that dominates their lives. They are not anxious to do ill; they have no great aspirations for good. If they were free agents, which they are not, they would prefer good to evil. But being good does not happen to fill their stomachs, but doing evil does, either in prison or in the lodging-houses.

Now, I myself will venture into psychology, and I will voice their opinions. "We are poor, weak and afflicted, but we are not to blame; no one will give us work, for we have had no training; we cannot do hard work, we are not big or strong enough; we do not want to be dishonest, but we must live somehow. If we are caught we go to prison, where we have food and lodgings and no hard work to do; and they are good to us in prison." This, I contend, is a fair statement of the condition and temperament of thousands that we call criminals!

Is it a wonder, then, I would ask, that many of them find their way into convict prisons, Portland, Parkhurst or Dartmoor, as their health permits?

What about Borstal! I hear some one say. The doors of Borstal are closed against them, for they are neither big enough, strong enough nor healthy enough for Borstal, which demands, and receives, strong, healthy young fellows only—no others need apply!

I have no doubt that the psychology of these fellows changes with the flight of years and frequent imprisonments, and probably when they arrive at forty years of age they will provide an interesting study for clever professors of psychology, though I am inclined to believe that even at that age their bodies will still be indexes to their mind, for their weaknesses and abnormalities will be the more pronounced.

Now, all this does not mean that I wish it to be inferred that healthy and well-developed men never commit crime, for that is far from true. Some of the worst rogues and most dangerous criminals I have ever met have been strong, handsome fellows, well over the average size of fully developed men. There are, however, so far as my experience has shown me, but few criminals of that description; though it is of course certain that big men may commit crimes of any kind, and healthy, handsome, educated men who persist in crime may well be subjects for psychological research; but of that class I shall have more to say in another chapter. For the present I am maintaining that physical causes determine the character and lives of the bulk of our criminals; that they are criminals not because they possess a dark, mysterious psychology, or because they are of malice aforethought determined to be criminals, but because they are either weak or afflicted.

In a word weakness, not wickedness, is the one general cause of crime.

These men form a stage army of criminals; they move from place to place; they are classified and catalogued in prison after prison; they are tossed from pillar to post; they are subjected to short terms of useless imprisonment and then thrust into short terms of hopeless liberty. What wonder that their physical condition gets worse! Or that they ultimately attain to certified feeble-mindedness!

Many of them, as I have pointed out, eventually commit serious crimes; and then a series of sentences to penal servitude await them, if happy death does not claim them or lunatic asylums absorb them.

The great majority, however, pursue their wearying round of small crimes and small imprisonments.

The State then discovers that, though they are not insane, not absolutely feeble-minded, that there is something wrong with them, and that they are, so to speak, "childish."

So a half-way classification has been coined for them; they are, the State declares, "unfit for prison discipline." Unfit for prison! unfit for asylums! unfit for liberty! unfit for social or industrial life! unfit for anything!

They are in a parlous state, they commit crime, but they are not criminals. Every year 400 new names are added to the list of these unfortunates who are still regularly committed to prison, so the Prison Commissioners tell us. Again I ask, what can it profit us to know more of the psychology of these "criminals" than is apparent to any one with eyes?

I am almost ashamed of calling attention to this national disgrace, I have done it so frequently; but I have called to deaf ears so far as this country is concerned. But I have some comfort in knowing that in one European country where my pamphlets on this question have been very largely distributed, a large piece of uncultivated land has been secured and a colony established for the permanent detention and complete segregation of these helpless people. To Holland, then, belongs the honour of being the first nation to make a merciful and sensible provision for this unfortunate class.

But I would like to ask our authorities whether they ever read their own Blue books! Whether they really do so, or carefully abstain from doing so, I would like them to read carefully and consider seriously the following extracts from the Prison

Commissioners' report for 1910-11, just issued. These extracts I give exactly in the same words used by the different prison officials. They speak for themselves, and all bear testimony to my contention that the physical condition of thousands of our prisoners is the root cause of their criminality.

Lancaster

"Forty-seven prisoners of weak intellect (thirty-six males and eleven females) were received during the year. Only the worst cases are here referred to. This useless procedure (the committal and recommittal of such people to prison) continues. No good purpose is served by it, except that these people receive perhaps better food and better treatment than they are accustomed to outside.

"They usually work well under supervision, and, except for occasional offences against the regulations (rather in the nature of silly pranks) they are fairly well behaved, orderly and respectful."

Holloway

"Forty-six prisoners on remand from police courts and petty sessions were reported insane. Two were found 'insane on arraignment,' and five 'guilty but insane.'

"No convicted prisoners were certified as insane at the prison. Thirty-two were classed as feeble-minded, 403 prisoners under remand were specially observed and examined as to their mental condition: 204 were remanded for this purpose."

Liverpool

"The number of epileptics was 92. Out of 167 prisoners remanded for mental observation, thirty-four males and ten females were found to be insane, and dealt with by summary jurisdiction.

"When prisoners are suspected by the Liverpool police of being weak-minded, they are remanded for mental observation, and on my confirmatory report are discharged to the workhouse or care of friends."

Wakefield

"It was found necessary to put 360 prisoners under mental observation, either on reception, or after location, in the general prison. The following are the details of 210 of the more marked and decided of these cases of mental defect—

    Reported weak-minded 66
    Certified as lunatics and removed to an asylum 9
    Epilepsy and allied conditions 53
    Prisoners with a past history of threatened or
    attempted suicide 15
    Temporary alcoholic excitement 67

"Last year the number of weak-minded was sixty, and of certified lunatics seven. It is interesting to observe how closely the figures now given approximate to those of last year."

Wormwood Scrubbs

"Twenty-six prisoners of markedly feeble mind were received (four of them were each committed twice and one of the number three times during the year), and the cases of thirty-five prisoners of this class were brought to the notice of the police prior to their discharge from prison.

"The chief defects noted were as follows—

(*a*) Physical deficiency and deformities   126 per 1000

(*b*) Mental deficiency   25   "   "

(*c*) Affections of heart, lung, and principal organs 129   "   "

(*d*) Visual defects   49   "   "

(*e*) Auditory defects   14   "   "

"They were regularly inspected at work, and their training and general well-being were closely supervised."

Feltham

"The very poor physique of the inmates on admission impresses one very much more than is shown by the figures of comparison with any so-called normal standards, as we do not separate our town and country inmates. Our country inmates, as a rule, have better physique, and though not so mentally quick are more hopeful cases when once a hold can be obtained of them. Among the town inmates one finds two classes, one showing signs of degeneration, as poor physique, narrow chest, short stature,

29

light weight associated with a low cunning and a peculiar restlessness of their eyes, watching for every movement; and among these a high arched palate is often noticed."

Borstal

"Although evil environment must of course take first place among the causes of most of these youths' downfall, I am becoming more and more struck with the importance of physical unfitness as a determining factor.

"From observations actually made among a large number of our older receptions, I find that some 60 per cent. had tried (some many times) to join either the Army or Navy. Only 15 per cent. of these had passed 'fit.' Many of the remaining 40 per cent., knowing that their physical defects would unfit them, had not been to a recruiting-office, so that presumably, but for physical inferiority we might have saved about one-half of those sentenced to the Borstal system."

Note.—The above remarks become the more striking when it is borne in mind that Borstal receives the best and healthiest young prisoners.

Parkhurst

"A new feature has been the formation of 'An Aged Convicts' Party' consisting of old men of sixty-seven years of age and upwards; they are located together, with special diet and privileges. A day room has been provided, also a garden with a yard adjoining; they are expected to do any light work they can undertake, without being tasked, and they are allowed to read and converse together. They appear to appreciate the relaxation of the ordinary prison discipline, and so far their behaviour has been excellent.

"The number classified as weak-minded at the end of the year was 120, but in addition there were twenty-seven convicts attached to the parties of weak-minded for further mental observation.

Classification of Weak-minded Convicts

    (*a*) Congenital deficiency—

        1. With epilepsy   10

        2. Without epilepsy   36

    (*b*) Imperfectly developed stage of insanity 26

    (*c*) Mental debility after attack of insanity 13

(*d*)	Senility	3
(*e*)	Alcoholic	9
(*f*)	Undefined	23
	Total	120

"The following is a list of crimes of the classified weak-minded, for which they are undergoing their present sentences of penal servitude, and the number convicted for each type of crime—

False pretences	1
Receiving stolen property	2
Larceny	24
Burglary	13
Shopbreaking, housebreaking, etc.	19
Blackmailing	1
Manslaughter	5
Inflicting grievous bodily harm	2
Wounding with intent	7
Shooting with intent	3
Wilful murder	10
Rape	2
Carnal knowledge of little girls	8
Arson	17
Horse-stealing	3

Killing sheep   1

Unnatural offence   1

Placing obstruction on railway   1

"A study of the criminal history of these 120 weak-minded convicts shows that sixty-two committed their first crime before the age of twenty years, and the total number of previous convictions standing against these 120 convicts amounted, in the aggregate, to 91 penal and 1,306 others. Forty convicts were certified insane: of these twenty-four were removed to the Criminal Asylum at Parkhurst, five to Broadmoor Asylum, seven to the County or Borough Asylums, one recovered, and three detained in the Prison Infirmary. Please notice how closely these figures approximate to the figures of the previous year."

Gloucester

(a)	The *bona fide* working men in search of employment	17	per cent.
(b)	The casual labourer unwilling or unfit for continued work—the first to lose employment and the last to regain it as trade falls or rises	31	"
(c)	The habitual vagrant and mendicant	41	"
(d)	Old and infirm persons "wandering to their own	11	"

hurt," crawling from ward to ward, entering the
workhouse infirmary only when compelled to do
so, living by begging, and constant trouble to the
police and magistrates

100

Pentonville

"As in former years the number, especially of youths,
imprisoned for minor—I will not say trivial—offences has been
considerable. What to do with these lads is a problem of much
difficulty, many are homeless and friendless. Their parents are
dead, or have forsaken their offspring; living just anywhere or
anyhow, one can only have for such a feeling of profound pity."

Wakefield

"The steadily increasing number of the vagrant and feeble-
minded is a subject urgently demanding special legislation. It is

34

hopeless for any Discharged Prisoners' Aid Society to attempt to do anything for these cases."

Wandsworth

"The weak-minded have been collected and reported in each case according to Standing Order. Sixteen cases of insanity were also dealt with."

Can any words of mine add force to these terrible statements and convincing figures? I think not! Can any master of the English language add potency to them? I think not! so I let them stand in their bald simplicity as a proof of my contention, and as an indictment of our present methods for dealing with smitten and afflicted prisoners.

CHAPTER III

IS THERE A CRIMINAL TYPE?

Is there a criminal type? After years of close observation, during which I have formed many friendships with criminals, I can only answer this question in the words that I have answered it before, and say that, physically, I have not found any evidence to show that a criminal type exists. In saying this I know that I shall run counter to the teaching of a good many people, and probably run counter to public opinion. For the criminal class and the criminal type have been written about so largely, and talked about so frequently, that the majority of people have come to the conclusion that our criminals come from a particular order of society, and that the poorest; or that there exists a type of people whose physical appearance gives outward and visible signs that proclaim the inward criminal mind.

I believe both these ideas to be entirely wrong. I was confirmed in my opinion last year when I visited many of the largest prisons in the United States; for I found there, as I have found in England, a complete absence among the prisoners of those physical and facial peculiarities that we are taught to believe differentiate criminals from ordinary citizens.

Speaking on this subject to the American Congress at Washington on October 4, 1910, Sir Evelyn Ruggles-Brise, K.C.B., the esteemed chairman of our Prison Commissioners, made the following statement—

"There is no criminal type. Nothing in the past has so retarded progress as the conviction, deeply rooted and widespread, that the criminal is a class by himself, different from all others, with a tendency to crime, of which certain peculiarities of body are the outward and visible signs.

"This superstition, for such I think it must be called, was, you know, strengthened and encouraged by the findings of the Italian school.

"It is not based upon disinterested and exact investigation, and not only has the progress of the science of criminal anthropology been retarded by this conception, but it accounts for the unfavourable and sceptical attitude which we still find in many places towards any attempt to reform the criminal.

"It is my own belief that the assumed co-relation between the mental and physical characteristics of a man is a superstition and fallacy. I do not believe that a murderer can be revealed by his frontal curve, or a thief by his bulging forehead or the shape of his nose. In England, we have been at great pains during the last two or three years to disprove, by scientific and exact investigations, this popular conception of a criminal. We have personally examined three thousand of our worst convicts, men sentenced to penal servitude and guilty of every form of crime. With regard to each we have collected and tabulated no less than ninety-six statements, that is, measurements, family history, mental and bodily characteristics, etc. The tabulation is now proceeding at the Biometric Laboratory, University College, London, under the direction of Dr. Karl Pearson. The results will be published shortly, and we are only able at present to say that so far no evidence whatever has emerged from this investigation confirming the existence of criminal types such as Lombroso and his disciples have asserted.

"And, in fact, both with regard to measurements and the presence of physical anomalies in criminals, these statistics present a startling conformity with similar statistics of the law-abiding. I thought it might interest this assembly to know that this investigation has been undertaken.

"Its results will be what most of us would have anticipated, but it will be a scientific result, and will serve to break down the vulgar superstition that criminals are a special type, and as such, in many cases beyond the reach of reform."

We await with some interest the declaration of results, but, too, I feel confident that no evidence will be forthcoming to prove that criminals can be detected by certain peculiarities of the head and face. Low foreheads, square jaws, scowling eyes, big, wide ears, and stubby beards do not denote criminality; receding foreheads, almost absence of chin and weak eyes do not indicate it either.

Emphatically I say that all these peculiarities may be quite consistent with honour and honesty, with industry and self-respect. Yet I am persuaded that all these things would tell against the unhappy prisoner, if he, although innocent, stood charged with serious crime.

And I am equally sure that if he were guilty, and the evidence proved him guilty, that his peculiarities would add very considerably to the length of his sentence. Sometimes a judge or magistrate will so far forget his dignity and say, alluding to the prisoner's appearance, "I can see the sort of man you are." And his sentence is measured accordingly.

On the other hand, the basest criminality is quite consistent with a well-shaped head, a well-developed body, a handsome face and a clear skin. Some of the most persistent, dangerous and unscrupulous criminals I have ever met have been fine, handsome men, accompanied either in the dock or out of it with fine-looking women.

Indeed, dangerous criminals are all the more dangerous when possessed of health and good looks. Yet I venture to say that health and beauty, when charged with serious and repeated crime, gets off with a much lighter sentence than affliction and ugliness! I have frequently known stupid, half-witted and repulsive-looking criminals far more severely dealt with than clever, dangerous rogues of more prepossessing appearance.

For the thick head does not interest us; the possessor does not excite our sympathy in the least. Nevertheless "thick head" may be far less guilty, far more worthy of compassion, and a much better fellow than the good-looking but complete scoundrel who does interest us. But his thick-headedness is against him; he is estimated and punished accordingly.

When standing in front of some hundreds of prisoners, all clothed in the depressing prison uniform, all exhibiting in their faces the well-known and easily recognised prison pallor, they all look pretty much alike, excepting those who suffer from deformities or physical deprivations. But closer observation and personal contact very quickly shows that the prisoners differ as much and as widely as ordinary citizens differ.

Could we remove their prison clothing, dress them as ordinary citizens dress, and mingle them with a mass of ordinary citizens, I venture to say that no scientist would be able to detect the criminals by the formation of their heads or the size of their ears. I do not maintain that men who possess queer-shaped heads do not commit crime. This is far from being the case. Unfortunately they do, and very serious crime too; but I do maintain that the perpetration of crime was caused not by the shape of their heads, but by causes that exist independently of it. We have, of course, a very large number of degenerates, but every degenerate does not possess an ill-formed head. Neither is every degenerate a criminal. Many of them are happy enough, and innocent enough when they can get enough to eat and places wherein to sleep. But when deprived of these things they may steal, beg, sleep out, or commit some other offence that brings them within the meshes of the law, and become criminals. They become criminals not because they possess criminal minds, but because there is no place for them in our social and industrial life; because their necessities cannot be supplied in any other way.

To classify such people as criminals is about as wise and just as classifying babes as criminals! Though they form a considerable proportion of our prison population, they are not to be detected by their ill-shaped heads, for some that are declared to be feeble-minded are quite up to the ordinary standard of beauty.

But there is another kind of degeneracy that cannot be mistaken, because it can be easily ascertained and established. I now refer to the physical measurements of prisoners. For many years it has been noted both in Europe and America that juvenile prisoners are much inferior in height, weight, muscular strength and capacity to the average height, weight and strength of the industrial population of similar age. Our own Prison Commissioners have for ten years conducted an examination in Pentonville prison of all prisoners between the ages of 16 years and 21 years. They have given us the results in words and figures that compel thought. Once more I give their words: "They are as a class two inches shorter and fourteen pounds lighter than the average industrial population of similar ages, and 28 per cent. of them suffer from some disease, affliction, or deprivation," and the Commissioners add that the highest proportion of reconvictions comes from among them, being no less than 40 per cent.

As nearly 1400 of such prisoners pass through Pentonville every year, and as, moreover, the examination extended over a series of years, it will be admitted that the results may be taken as not only correct with regard to Pentonville, but taken also as an accurate description of our youthful prisoners generally, so far as large towns are concerned.

I am permitted to visit Pentonville and other prisons frequently for the purpose of addressing the prisoners, so that I see prisoners in the bulk, and I see many of them separately too.

I am persuaded that the findings of the medical authorities of that particular prison give a pretty accurate description of prisoners generally. Retarded growth, ill-nourished bodies and general weakness have a thousand times more to do with crime than ill-shaped heads. Over the causes of the latter we have no control, but over the causes that lead to stunted and ill-nourished bodies we may have, and ought to have, complete control.

But the great bulk of them have not criminal minds, and though a very limited number of them show a tendency to deeds of passion or cruelty, the vast majority find their way into prison simply because they are helpless outside prison. They must eat, drink and sleep, and to procure these things they follow the line of least resistance, and beg or steal.

Their lack of stature, wisdom and muscle renders them incapable of contending with their more robust fellows, for industrial life demands either technical skill or robust health; having neither, they are crowded out of every occupation.

Such men form a great proportion of our prisoners, but they present a problem that the sociologist rather than the

Psychologist is called upon to solve, for they are the direct product of defective social, economic, industrial, educational and domestic conditions. To sociologists, then, I point out these things in the hope that more attention will be given to them, for it will be an ill day for us if the serious interest and attention of England is diverted from causes, and concentrated on effects.

It does not of course follow that because a man is below the normal height and weight that he is necessarily a weakling, for many little men are marvels of virility and physique, possessing great brain power and convincing personality. Of such men I have nothing to say excepting that when one does become a criminal, he is likely to be a clever and determined criminal. As I search my mind, and bring to my memory the numerous criminals that I have associated with, I am conscious of the fact that nearly all the clever, determined and successful were small-sized men, light of step, quick of action, upright in carriage, of good appearance. But they possessed plenty of vitality, their eyes did not betray them, neither did their heads, ears or chins "give them away."

Four of the most complete burglars I ever knew were men of this stamp. Three of them are now in prison, and though the fourth sometimes comes to see me and produces evidence to show that he is getting a decent living, I shall not be surprised if he too suddenly disappears. One of the cleverest, coolest and most perfect criminals I ever knew was of very small size, straight in body if crooked in mind. While I am persuaded that physically there exists no such thing as a criminal type, I am still more persuaded that socially there exists no such thing as a "criminal class."

Real crime exists altogether apart from bodily conformation or from social standing. It may be said, and with truth, that the prison population is largely recruited from the ranks of the poor. But it must be borne in mind that the great mass of the people are poor, many of them being very poor. The number of the rich or well-to-do is but small compared with the number of poor.

It is quite natural, then, that the bulk of prisoners should come from the class that overwhelmingly predominates. If the numbers of affluent and the poor could be exactly ascertained, I believe that it would be found that the poor do not contribute more than a proportionate share of the country's criminals.

Poverty itself is but rarely a decisive factor in the perpetration of crime, though environment is. In poor countries crime is not rampant, for Ireland, the poorest of the British Isles, shows a much lower ratio of crime than England, Scotland or Wales. Even in the terrible slums of London, where the poverty is intense, where misery and suffering abound, where thousands of men and women are but a single day in advance of starvation, where absolute destitution is always in evidence, the number of real and confirmed criminals does not exceed a fair proportion when the number of the inhabitants are taken into consideration. I feel bound to say this much for the very poor in our London slums. During many years' close acquaintance, I have found them to be as law-abiding and honest as any portion of the community in proportion to numbers. When their environment and temptations are considered, their rectitude, to me, is a matter of great wonder.

There are criminals amongst them, but after all they are the exceptions, and the worst criminals that are amongst them are those who have descended from higher social stations.

Man for man and woman for woman, my experience has taught me that slum-dwellers are not below the average population in honesty and industry.

I say this appears marvellous at first thought, but in reality it is not so, for wealth and leisure are not unmixed blessings. Probably they are as likely to produce criminals, or even more so, than poverty and care. The criminal ranks, then, are by no means recruited from the poor alone, for all classes and every station contribute their proportion.

To speak of the very poor as the "criminal classes" is wrong and misleading. The term can only be applicable to the blighted, helpless weaklings constantly in prison, who have neither wit, courage, nor strength to conceive and carry out anything approaching organised crime. These, it must be admitted, come largely from the poor, for they are the product of poverty. The term might also be used with regard to men and women who live by organised crime, and who mean to live by crime: who, despising and refusing every respectable mode of life, apply their talents, energy, courage, presence of mind, knowledge of business, society and social custom to the one purpose of their lives.

To such men and women no other life has the slightest attraction. Comfortable ease to them is monotonous, and to them honest persevering endeavour, though successful, has no charms. Of this class the poor furnish but few, but every station of life, not excluding the Church and the universities, contributes more or less, for concerted crime demands more knowledge than the poor possess.

Swindling, to be successful, must be done on a large scale, and requires exact knowledge. Forgery demands skill and education. Long firms, bogus company promoting and blackmailing require characteristics and knowledge that the poor do not possess. Jewel-thieves and pickpockets that operate at high-class functions have not graduated in the slums, but in more respectable life. But these men are real criminals, dangerous and persistent criminals; they plan and scheme, pursue and wait for the accomplishment of a criminal object. Decidedly they form a criminal class, yet, singular to say, they do not largely come from what are termed the "criminal classes."

I would like to pursue what I believe would prove a very interesting inquiry, so I ask: In what way do the crimes of the poor and ignorant differ from the crimes committed by those who have been educated and once possessed social standing?

Briefly, leaving out murder, the crimes of the poor and ignorant are burglaries, larcenies, assaults, felonies, wilful damage, vagabondage; while to the educated swindling, conspiracy, long firms, bogus companies, forgeries, and blackmailing may be attributed. If we compare the two lists for one moment only, we see that the crimes of the educated classes reveal malice aforethought, and betray criminal mind and intention.

Impulsive or instinctive crimes, and crimes of passion, are more numerous amongst the ignorant than the educated. But such crimes do not betray a long-drawn-out criminal intention. The exigencies of the moment, sudden passion or temptation, momentary folly and the influence of drink account for most of the crimes committed by the ignorant. But these things do not conduce in any marked degree to the commission of crime by educated people; as I have said, their crime is generally pre-planned, not instinctive! Probably the proportion of criminals per number of men and women who comprise the different stations of life is about the same for every rank, though I am sure that the statement will be considered absolute heresy.

But it must be remembered that rich criminals are more likely to escape detection, arrest and punishment than the criminals of the poor. They are still more likely to plan numerous transactions that technically do not come within the meshes of criminal law, but which morally are as dishonest and rascally as any crime against property can possibly be. The ethics of commercial life are more than strange, for a bogus company promoter would probably be appalled should his son be charged with forgery or burglary, or his daughter with obtaining goods by false pretences. It is not, then, to be wondered at, that considering how many educated men are engaged in ventures that are financially unsound and morally bankrupt, that a number of them step over the line that divides the domain of civil jurisdiction from the province of criminal law.

The real wonder is that a great many more do not take that step.

After all, it seems a wise arrangement for the sorrows,

difficulties and temptations of life to be evenly distributed amongst the rich and the poor, the educated and the ignorant, though, to be sure, the ignorant are more likely to get within the meshes of the law, not because of their inherent criminality, but because of their ignorance which does not enable them to be dishonest without suffering the penalty. It is, I am sure, good for us that socially there exists no criminal class. I am glad that probity and honesty of life are not the monopoly of education and wealth, and I am also glad that if criminals we must have, that the rich and educated should furnish a proportionate share. The very poor have enough to bear and to suffer without having exclusive right to the shame and suffering that always attend discovered criminality. And it is well that no one section of the community can lift up its hands and proclaim its innocence. But all this leads me to say that there is no criminal class.

CHAPTER IV

EPILEPSY AND CRIME

In the extracts that I have given from prison officials' reports we learn that a considerable number of epileptics are detained in prison as criminals. During 1910-11 the figures for three prisons were as follows: Liverpool 92; Wakefield 53; and Parkhurst 10. In three prisons only we had, then, during one year 155 proved epileptics undergoing imprisonment, ten of whom were sentenced to penal servitude. I call particular attention to this matter, for it demands attention; 155 unfortunates, for whom out of sheer pity we ought to provide loving care, were thrust into prison, tabulated as criminals, and compelled to undergo the wearying monotony of prison life.

Undoubtedly epilepsy produces many serious crimes. This dread affliction, half physical and half mental, can induce a state of mind from which not only crimes of violence and of homicidal tendency may be the result, but crimes of almost any character.

Mental stupor, and sometimes complete aberration, follows or precedes epileptic seizures. Assaults, wilful damage, attempted murder, attempted suicide, thefts, indecency and criminal assaults, as well as murder itself, are quite likely to be committed. I have, in fact, personally known such crimes committed, some of them repeatedly, by well-known epileptics. I have been a frequent visitor in houses where some member of the family was an epileptic. I had, perhaps, met the sufferer in the cells, or the friends had been to consult the magistrate, and I had called upon them in consequence. The public generally have no idea of the extent to which epilepsy prevails. I have no figures or statistics to give; I do not know whether or not it is on the increase, though, if I had to give an opinion, I should say it was.

I know it is very common. I know an epileptic is one of the most woeful objects on earth; I know the anxiety and sorrow of families who have one such in their homes. I know that many, very many serious crimes and a world of suffering might be saved if we had registration of, and proper provision for epileptics.

The provision made for these unfortunates is miserably insufficient. Their neglect by the State is a national scandal, but it is also a public danger. People who can pay may have their epileptics cared for. But the epileptics of the poor are cared for by short periods of confinement in prison, workhouse or asylum. We have a right to ask for some large, considerate and humane method of treating epileptics, for a wise nation would protect them against themselves, and would protect society against them; and would remove that dreadful anxiety that depresses so many people who have an epileptic among them: the fear of "something happening."

One would think it impossible in these days for a man to be continually sentenced to imprisonment because he suffers from epilepsy, yet such is undoubtedly the case. I have no personal knowledge of the 155 epileptics detained in the three prisons I have quoted; but I have personal knowledge and prolonged experience of many sufferers whom I have seen sent to prison for offences committed in the throes of their frightful affliction.

One of the finest fellows, physically, I have ever known was a hopeless epileptic. He had served with distinction in a famous cavalry regiment in India; he suffered from sunstroke, and as the affects were serious and prolonged he was invalided from the Army. He recovered somewhat, and married, but when children were born to him epilepsy developed. I have seen the horror that ensued in his home: the fears of his wife, the terror of his children, but I realised most of all the pitiful condition of the man himself. Many times I have in his own home taken part, at some risk to myself, in restraining him from violence, and when sometimes our efforts have been unavailing, the police have been called in, and I have seen him conveyed to the police station, and from there to the police court. When in the dock, standing charged with violence and assaults, I have seen a fit come upon him, when half a dozen policemen would be required to straighten him out upon the floor and to hold him till stupor supervened, when his spell of violence would give way to insensibility and heavy, stertorous breathing.

I have seen his wife and children standing weeping in the court. Out of sheer pity I have known a kind and wise magistrate sentence him to six months' imprisonment without hard labour: for he felt that for six months at any rate the man, the wife and children would be protected.

None the less the poor fellow felt the indignity and cruelty of his position, and whenever committed to prison he never failed to communicate with the Home Secretary, and petition for release. In the pigeon-holes of the Home Office I have no doubt many of this man's letters and appeals are carefully stored.

But unfortunately when epileptics marry the evil and suffering does not end with them, for when children are born, they often prove very strange beings.

I have watched the growth of such children; I have seen their strange whims and their oft-times irresponsibility. I have known the girls become hopelessly immoral and cleverly dishonest even at their school age. One of the cleverest thieves I ever knew was a girl of fourteen, whose father was an epileptic. She looked the picture of confiding innocence, but she robbed and cheated all sorts of people: doctors and clergymen were her special prey.

She was charged repeatedly; no reformatory would receive her, for she was flagrantly immoral. At sixteen she was a drab and a sleeper-out; at eighteen she became an inmate of a lunatic asylum, but at twenty her life came mercifully to an end.

I have watched the progress of boys born to an epileptic mother or father, and again, they are strange beings. I have not found them to be the equal of girls in lying or dishonesty, but I have found them to be idle and shiftless; incapable of giving sustained attention to study or work; sometimes becoming drunkards and vagrants before the days of full manhood were reached.

So far as my experience goes, I have not found that the children of an epileptic suffer from "fits" or manifest seizures. They do not bear on their bodies the cuts, wounds and bruises that are often found on the bodies of those who do suffer, but I have found, and certainly my experience does not stand alone, that they are often irresponsible creatures possessing strange minds, clever in certain directions and those directions not for good; capable of serious crime, but never exhibiting any sorrow, fear or remorse when convicted of any offence. They generally insist upon their absolute innocence, but go to prison just as unconcernedly as they would go elsewhere.

Not very long ago a wealthy gentleman wrote to me about his daughter, a beautiful and accomplished woman of twenty-two. He told me that she had been in prison and was again in the hands of the police, charged with fraud. His letter led to an interview; he candidly told me that his daughter had been untruthful and dishonest for many years, but now he was ashamed to say that she was grossly immoral.

He had been compelled to remove her from every educational establishment in which she had been placed, for her lies and dishonesty could not be tolerated. He had placed her with more than one private governess, but while she made excellent progress with her studies, and especially with music, even for liberal payment no one could be found to give her a home and supervision beyond a very short period.

The grief and shame of both father and mother were apparent; their daughter being in the hands of the police, they knew that I could not save her; but they wanted some hope and some guidance for the future. "Can nothing be done?" they repeatedly asked. I could give them but little comfort; I dared not create hope, for I had learned during our conversation that the mother herself suffered at intervals, sometimes longer and sometimes shorter, from epileptic "fits." In my heart I felt sure that this was the real cause of the daughter's strange behaviour; I did not, however, add to their sorrow by telling them what I thought.

My experience of epileptics has been much larger than the ordinary run of my life would lead any one to imagine, for outside my police court and prison experience I have had frequent opportunities for gaining knowledge and forming judgment. Probably few men have a more varied post-bag than myself; rightly or wrongly, large numbers of people believe that I can give them advice or help in family and other matters.

So all sorts of difficulties and sorrows are placed before me. But most of my correspondents consult me about some member of their family who is at once their despair and shame. Under such circumstances, I have always been ready to give such guidance and comfort as was possible. But being of inquiring mind, I always wanted to know the cause of the evil and sorrow. So I made inquiries regarding family history, etc., and was often brought face to face with the fact that father or mother, sometimes grandfather or grandmother, suffered from "fits."

Some years ago, after writing in the daily press upon the dangers of epilepsy, I received a large number of letters from friends of epileptics. Every post brought me letters which came from various parts of the country.

Most of my correspondents were in good financial positions, but their letters formed pitiful reading. A more dolorous collection it would be impossible to imagine. But they taught me a great deal, for I realised that this terrible affliction prevailed to a greater extent than I had dreamt of. I realised how respectable people cover and hide the fact of epilepsy as long as possible, and that when the fact can be no longer hidden they cower with shame, as if their sorrow was in itself a disgrace and a scandal. I had ample confirmation in those dolorous letters that not only pain, suffering, injury and hopelessness dwelt in the home of an epileptic; but also that shame, crime, imprisonment, strange actions and more than strange minds were some of the resultant effects. I need not dilate upon the danger to the public when large numbers of persons suffering from this malady are at liberty amongst them, for epileptic seizures may occur at any place and at any time. In a crowded street, or on a busy railway platform they might easily be attended with disaster. To any one who thinks upon this matter the danger will be apparent. But the dangers arising from the many individuals who have inherited a dread birthright, because they are born of epileptic parentage, are not so readily seen. None the less, those dangers are real and tangible, and I verily believe that if the truth could be ascertained regarding the large number of motiveless crimes for which the perpetrators have not been brought to justice, it would be found that very largely they were the outcome of epilepsy.

I take the following from the daily press of November 11, 1911—

"MURDERER'S LOST MEMORY

"UNCONSCIOUS OF CRIME FOR FOUR DAYS

"STRANGE DEFENCE

"Complete loss of memory was the unavailing defence at Nottingham yesterday, when Victor Chapman, a smart young ex-Lancer, was sentenced to death for the murder of Ralph Hill, whom he had shot in the Market-Place.

"Giving evidence on his own behalf prisoner declared that from nine o'clock on the morning of the crime, till he found himself at Divine Service in gaol four days later, he had not the faintest recollection of what had happened to him. He denied that he had the slightest desire to harm Hill, or that he had threatened him. Prisoner further stated he had a similar seizure last Whitsuntide.

"He left work at Nottingham at midday, and the next thing he remembered was looking at the Corn Exchange at Grimsby. He had no money, and walked back to Nottingham, reaching home three days later, exhausted and with bleeding feet.

56

"Nor could he recollect that two days prior to the crime (as a witness had sworn) he went to the river side, fired a shot into the air, and declared that he was going to shoot Hill and his (prisoner's) sweetheart.

"Dr. Owen Taylor, police surgeon, said when arrested prisoner had a strange expression, and appeared utterly indifferent to everything going on around him. "He betrayed no excitement, and during the whole of the time witness questioned him he stared witness straight in the face with a fixed and vacant expression."

"Two days later his condition vastly improved, he answered more quickly and brightly, and knew that he was accused of murder.

"Witness tested him in every possible way, but he had not the slightest remembrance of anything that happened on the fateful day.

"Pressed by the Judge to give an opinion, witness said it was possible that while suffering from an epileptic seizure, prisoner did not know what he was doing.

"The jury found prisoner guilty, and sentence of death was passed."

Instances similar to the above can easily be multiplied, but I content myself with one more case of recent date. The following appeared in the daily press of November 15, 1911—

"In charging the Grand Jury at the Stafford assizes yesterday, Mr. Justice Pickford referred to the case of Karl Kramer, who was arraigned for the triple murder at Kidsgrove. His Lordship pointed out that during the magisterial inquiry there seemed to be considerable doubt as to prisoner's sanity, and the magistrates adjourned the case sine die. A verdict of "Wilful Murder" was returned against him by the Coroner's Jury, and he did not think the jury would have any hesitation in finding that there was a prima facie case against the prisoner. When, later, Kramer was carried into court, he seemed in a state of collapse.

"Sir Richard Brayn, Home Office expert, in his evidence, said he examined the prisoner in Stafford Gaol on September 28. Questions were put to him, but no response could be elicited. Kramer's body and head were bent forward, and the only movement was a twitching of his right forefinger. He was in a state of rigidity the whole time.

"He had examined Kramer several times since, and had applied a test as to his sensibility, but the results were entirely negative. He formed the opinion that the prisoner was quite incapable of exercising his mental faculties in any way.

"Dr. Smith, medical officer at Stafford Prison, confirmed Sir Richard Brayn's evidence.

"The Judge: 'I suppose you both looked carefully to see

if the prisoner was shamming?' 'Oh, yes, I am entirely of the opinion that he was not shamming.'

"Kramer was found to be insane, and was ordered to be detained during his Majesty's Pleasure."

In addition to epileptics and the insane there exists a number of people, male and female, who present to those who know them a more pitiful and hopeless problem than the altogether mad, for the altogether mad are at any rate restrained and protected.

The men and women of whom I now speak suffer from some kind of mental disease that has not yet been classified, but which prevails to a much larger extent than the public is aware.

This disease does not prevent them following their ordinary occupations. Indeed, many of them are regular and indomitable workers, and it is probable that the great interest they have in their occupations prevents them becoming certifiably insane. Such men and women continue for years at their places of business or in their situations, conducting their affairs in an efficient manner; to their companions they appear quiet and decent people, though a little sombre.

But very different is the impression produced on those who unfortunately know them at home! Released from the engrossing interest of business, their mental and moral condition becomes apparent. Of all the sorrow and misery that I have seen in the sorrowful world in which I have lived and moved, I have seen no more woeful spectacle than the sight they present— objects at once pathetic, terrifying and hopeless. While all sorts of imaginings occupy their minds, some great delusion seems to dominate them and to destroy every atom of home comfort. Place them under authority, surround them with medical officers, question them and cross-question them, examine them and re-examine them, watch them unceasingly and they defy every member of the faculty to find traces of insanity.

Under such circumstances they can control their thoughts and speech; to a certain extent they can make the worst appear the better reason.

Only at liberty, when free of all control, is their condition made manifest. Sometimes they appear to have a feeling that mentally all is not quite right with them, but this feeling is but momentary, and soon disappears in the overmastering belief in the altogether imaginary wrongs they suffer at the hands of their friends.

I have known a not inconsiderable number of such men, and I have been worried for years with the imaginary troubles of such women. Argument is of no avail, no amount of proof convinces them of their error. Years go on, during which they hug their delusion and terrify their families and friends. Sometimes the delusion appears but a little harmless eccentricity, nevertheless it dominates and damns the man's domestic life. At other times the grievance is more serious, often taking shape in the belief of a faithful and devoted wife's infidelity. The horror and suffering in an otherwise good home, when this delusion is the master-belief of a husband and father, cannot be portrayed, for it is past the power of words. I have seen it again and again, and have felt my impotence when I tried to comfort and protect the innocent wife, and still more when I have tried to argue with and dissuade the husband.

The behaviour of such men is both maddening and heart-breaking; sometimes it continues for years, and the home gradually becomes a hopeless hell. Sometimes when a spell of passion and violence has been particularly exhaustive, I have known it followed with a period of almost stupor, forgetfulness and absolute irresponsibility. Crimes of violence, suicide or attempted suicide sometimes result. In the latter case the law has no scruple in doing what ought to have been done years before, for then it proclaims the man's irresponsibility. It is, however, but cold comfort to the wife or friends to find the law, which had refused to acknowledge the man's irresponsibility while he lived, so ready to proclaim it when he was dead, for the fact might with some advantage have been discovered much sooner.

I have said that sometimes in a lucid moment the possibility of becoming insane dawns upon them; when it does, their horror is great and their suffering intense.

I have sat beside such men as they lay in bed, I have watched the expression on their faces, and I have listened to heavy breathing, for words they had none. I have seen them rise from bed in a state of stupor and do some foolish or childish thing. I have been ignored as if I were not present, and I have been made aware of the strange fact that maddening excitement had been followed by the suspension of mental faculties. I have known men in this condition wander from home into the streets, where a special Providence seemed to care for them and protect them from serious accident. Frequently men of this description are arrested by the police and charged with violence or disorderly conduct. Sometimes the magistrate, noticing their strange behaviour, remands them and asks the medical officer at the prison to examine and report upon them. Invariably the report is to the effect that the prisoners have shown no indication of insanity. The detention during remand is generally considered sufficient punishment, but an admonition from the Bench on the evils of drink very often precedes the prisoner's discharge.

Back to their homes they go, confirmed in their delusions and made more bitter by their arrest and detention. Especially is this the case when a long-suffering wife has herself appealed to the police for protection. It is small wonder that some of these unfortunate men are eventually executed for wife murder.

CHAPTER V

WOMEN AND CRIME

It is well known that even educated and well-to-do women are sometimes afflicted with what, for want of a better word, I will call "acquisitiveness," though some people call it "kleptomania." Under the power of this mania, vice or habit women become positively helpless, bringing disgrace upon their respectable friends, and ruin upon themselves.

A pitiful problem they present. People smile incredulously about them. Judges and magistrates sometimes inform the culprits, and the public, that they sit in court for the purpose of curing this habit, vice or crime. And an admiring public always endorses, and acclaims the heavy sentence of imprisonment awarded.

But neither judge nor magistrate can cure it, for a sentence of five years' penal servitude given by a judge is quite as futile as a sentence of three months' imprisonment given by a magistrate. Women of this kind exist among the poor even as they do among the rich, and they are just as responsible as acquisitive jackdaws. They steal, store up, and hide all sorts of portable articles, and, like jackdaws, they make no use of the articles stolen.

But their lives are drawn-out tragedies, for they, in spite of, or because of numerous imprisonments, dwell long in the land. Not long since, an old woman of eighty-one was again sent to three years' penal servitude for what was termed "shoplifting." She had stolen a number of trifles from a well-known establishment. The old woman was comparatively rich; she owned house property; she had some hundreds of pounds standing to her credit in a bank, and she had also considerable investments. When free of prison she lived alone. When the police searched her rooms, some hundreds of articles were discovered hidden away in all sorts of queer places. The old woman's bed was made far from comfortable by the presence of hair-brushes, combs, hand-glasses, etc. In other places were ribbons, gloves, tooth-brushes, and bits of cloth carefully stored. It was stated that there was no evidence to prove that she had either used, sold or given away any of the articles, or in any way made use of the things stolen.

Am I wrong in saying that prison was the wrong place for the old woman? Ought not restraining and protecting care to have been provided for her in some other place, and her means utilised to allow her suitable comforts? But while there are numbers of similar women dragging out their weary lives in prison, there are still a greater number in whom the passion or habit of stealing is but a passing phase, and who pay a heavy penalty for belonging to the female sex. I have in my mind a large number of girls, ages varying from twelve to twenty years. Scores of mothers have consulted me about such girls, and probably hundreds still consult our magistrates. Many of those girls were disobedient and apparently wicked. Some of them were inveterate thieves, and some, even at fourteen, were addicted to vice. I have seen numbers of them charged with stealing. But they never knew why they had stolen; some of them did not even know what they had done with the stolen articles.

When in the dock or cells they behaved in a passive, bewildered way, exhibiting no anxiety or concern. Many girls of this character became a kind of charge to me, and I visited them and their parents repeatedly.

At home I found them strange creatures, upon whom good advice and kind words produced no effect. Sometimes I have given advice to their mothers; at other times I have paid for medical advice, which has occasionally brought about the desired result.

But many of them I have seen charged again and again till they found their way into reformatories or prison.

Now these girls were not thieves, although they had stolen. In most of them there was no real vice, although they were to all appearance vicious. But owing to sexual causes a state of body and mind existed that rendered them incapable of sound judgment or self-control, and liable at any time to yield to vicious impulses.

To associate girls of this description in rescue homes or reformatories with the hardened and the wicked is a sure way to demoralisation. It ought to be possible, in these enlightened days, to find some sensible way of dealing with such children. What they require is the fatherly doctor and the enlightened motherly matron; nourishing food, fresh air, healthy exercise and innocent recreation combined may save many of them. Failing these conditions these girls must and will become criminals, or drabs, most probably both. But similar causes operate with serious consequences on older women. Consider, if you please, the life of a poor married woman in London. If she has no children, she suffers untold physical and mental torture, if she has children they come all too often. The constant fluctuations of her system, the constant depression of mind, the same four little walls everlastingly to look at, the same eternal anxiety as to the future, the trying and continued worry with the children, the usual lack of sympathy from the husband, and the same vile air to breathe over and over again make her life almost unbearable.

Men who have a constant change of scene little know what gloomy imaginings prey upon her; they little know what nameless terrors haunt her. For months before a child is born many of these women are not really rational. To make some provision for the coming "trouble" they steal; but the inconsequence of their action is proved by the fact that many of them steal things that are of no earthly use to them.

Of our London magistrates we are justly proud, and to me it is a matter of profound thankfulness to know that any one of them will break the letter of the law, if by so doing he can perform an act of mercy to an unfortunate woman. But woman's troubles are long dragged out. Early womanhood and the time of motherhood being passed, there comes a more trying physical and mental strain. At this time many seek relief by taking drink. True, it is a mistake, but who can wonder at it? Again, ill-health and nameless fears haunt the woman. Perhaps through it all she is to be found daily at charing work, and, in moving about the house in which she is working, temptations are presented to her, temptations that in her then state of mind and body it is impossible for her to resist.

So she steals, is prosecuted and sent to prison. I have a mental picture-gallery full of such women. "An honester woman never walked!" many a bewildered husband has said to me.

In spite of "acquisitiveness" and the prevalence of sexual disturbance, it is comforting to find that the honesty of women has for some years past become increasingly evident. It stands to their credit that while they considerably outnumber men, their proportion of crime is less than one-fourth of the whole. Were it not for the homeless and abandoned women of the streets, who are so frequently convicted, the honesty and sobriety of the women of England would be still more evident.

In London, one prison only is sufficient to meet all the demands that women create for prison detention; and that one is maintained very largely for the class of women who live upon the streets, the majority of whom ought to be permanently detained. This low proportion of crime among women is the more remarkable from the fact that for many years past a large and increasing number of them have entered into the labour market, and have been exposed to many (but not all) temptations to which men are exposed.

I say this the more readily and cheerfully, because it has become quite the fashion in certain quarters to describe the women of England as increasingly drunken; a statement that cannot be possibly substantiated.

At any rate they are increasingly honest, and were it not for the causes to which I have alluded, our prisons would be practically free from women.

I know that the Society for the Prevention of Cruelty to Children has a necessary and an active existence, and I know that I can be overwhelmed with their facts and figures; I also know that cruelty to a child is one of the worst possible crimes; I know all this, but I know more also, for I know that the great bulk of English mothers or matrons that are committed to prison on this account are more fit for asylums and mental treatment than they are for prison and penal discipline. They demand pity instead of punishment, the doctor and the nurse instead of the governor and the warder; medicine and fresh air instead of cellular confinement.

Most of them are poor, helpless creatures, weak of mind and weak of body; quite incapable of looking after themselves, still more incapable of caring for and training children. I have seen the dirt and misery of many women, and the hopelessness of their lives long before they were committed to prison. I have helped to renew their homes, and have clothed the children while the feeble-minded mothers were in prison. But when those mothers came back, bringing their helplessness and irresponsibility with them, I have had the mortification of witnessing those homes and children sink back again to the old conditions. For neither warning nor imprisonment has the least effect upon such poor creatures.

But there is another class of women who are charged with this offence: women that seem possessed with an incarnate spirit of cruelty; who perpetrate fiendish cruelties upon children, or upon unfortunate little serving-maids; cruelties that are certain to be discovered and punished; cruelties that can neither bring pleasure nor profit if they remain undiscovered. These cruelties are not the result of impulsive passion, for they are long persisted in. They form, it would appear, part and parcel of their ordinary life.

I want to say a word for these women! Does any one in their heart of hearts doubt the madness of such women! If so, let me say that my experience has taught me that they are as certainly mad as the veriest madman locked in any lunatic asylum. I have known some of them, and I have taken some measure of their madness.

Some day we shall have decent pity on the uncertified, unclassified but the undoubtedly mad.

But that will be when we are able to distinguish between disease and crime!

When that time comes, prison will no longer be the one and only specific for the cure of poverty and feeble-mindedness, mania and disease when criminal actions result from these afflictions. But judging from present procedure, that day is still a long way off.

CHAPTER VI

PRISONS—WHY THEY FAIL!

It is generally admitted that prison life, with its discipline and punishments, very largely fails to reform or deter those that are submitted to it.

The reasons are not far to seek. The very fact of a number of men, who are prone to commit certain actions, being detained in prison, makes it certain that many of them will again commit those actions when they are again restored to liberty. For with liberty comes the temptation of opportunity, and with opportunity the fall.

Moral strength cannot be developed in the absence of temptation, for moral qualities must be free or die!

Prisons are at their best but unnatural places; for though the machinery, discipline and even the spirit that animates the whole of the officials be of the very best, still goodness, manhood, honesty and sobriety cannot grow inside a prison wall.

Doubtless tens of thousands of good resolutions are formed in prison. To many prisoners it seems impossible that they should repeat the actions that brought about their imprisonment when once more they are free. But they do repeat them, again and again. Prison life, then, neither deters nor reforms. But it does other things: it deadens, demoralises, or disgusts according to the temperament and characteristics of the individual prisoner.

The fixed belief in the virtue and necessity of prison has had disastrous consequences, for the State has hitherto considered it the one great cure-all for law-breaking. It has till quite recently been the first resource of the law, instead of its last resource, when called upon to deal with its erring children.

Roughly, the men and women who inhabit our prisons may be classified under five heads: First: the feeble-minded; second: the physical weaklings; third: the vagrant; fourth: the casual offender; fifth: the habitual offender. I believe that all our prisoners can be placed in one or more of these divisions, though of course there are variations. Should this be approximately the case, it is certain that a tremendous difficulty arises when the discipline and routine of any one prison, however well conducted, is made to serve for the whole of the classes.

This is where prisons fail, and must continue to fail if the present methods are continued, for in our endeavours to administer equal justice to all classes, we commit the greatest injustice; and in our attempts to be merciful, we are cruel to many of our prisoners.

For the feeble-minded, the weaklings, the vagrants and the habituals, prison has no terrors. To them it is at once a sanatorium and a lodging-house, as necessary for their health and personal cleanliness as quarantine is for those smitten of the plague.

To them the bath and the change of clothing, the clean cell, and the regular food are comforts, even refinement. But to the casual offender such things may be sickening and maddening beyond endurance.

To the former, the semi-idleness of prison, which makes no demand on their physical and mental powers, is grateful and comforting. To the man of industry, brain, imagination and culture this idle monotony is exasperating to a degree, unless he be endowed with philosophical stoicism.

The effect of prison discipline, then, is determined not by the rules and routine of any particular prison, but by the temperament of the individual under detention.

This failure to reform must not be attributed, then, to prison system altogether, still less must it be attributed to any lack of sympathy in the prison officials; but rather to the two facts, that prisons are unnatural places, and that a prison population is made up of strange and motley individuals, each differing widely from his fellows in temperament and taste, in physical and mental capacity.

An educated and refined man, one who loves liberty and social life, must of necessity find prison a terrible place. Should he be of a nervous, imaginative or morbid temperament, he suffers the torments of Hell. He knows in his heart that he has been a fool, probably he is never tired of reminding himself of the fact; but he gets no comfort from his knowledge, it adds no reasonableness to his disposition. He reviews his life again and again, not with feelings of shame or sorrow, but for the purpose of finding some excuse for himself or fixing some blame upon others.

He is full of fear for the future, but he has no sorrow for the past; he has no desire to undo the wrong he has done, no particular desire to avoid such wrongs in the future.

He lives in a state of chronic irritation; he is morose or excitable by turns. He does not find the officials sympathetic or courteous, for they, too, are human, and even in prison like meets with like.

The sufferings of these men are intense. The iron enters into their souls—and though their sufferings are largely self-created, they are none the less real.

Ask such a man to give a description of prison life, and he will give one worthy of Charles Reade.

But suppose we ask a different type of man to give us his opinion; he may be equally well educated with the former, he may have served a similar sentence in the same prison at the same time, none the less, he will present us with a striking contrast.

He will tell you that the prison was dull and monotonous, but just what he expected; that the food was unpleasant, till he got used to it; that many things disgusted him in his early prison days, but he put up with them. He kept all the rules, got all his "marks," and obtained full remission of sentence. In a word, he made the best of things.

He will tell you that he had no real work to do; that the officials were all good to him, but they had their duty to perform, and that he never insulted them. There was nothing of much interest going on, and that in reality formed his punishment, for he had many interests in the outside world.

Let me select another; this man may be considered an authority, for although he is under sixty years of age, his sentences amount to more than forty years. He knows Portland, Dartmoor, Parkhurst and, of course, many local prisons. He has had as much as fifteen years at a stretch, and as I understand he is again in prison, it is quite possible that ultimately (unless Mr. Gladstone's Preventive Detention Act takes possession of him), the accumulation of his sentences may outnumber the years of his life.

For he, too, got all his "marks" and has never failed to get three months off every year served.

There is not an idle bone in his body; he is industrious, skilled and intelligent; he loves liberty; to him the song of the birds and the smiling of the flowers are pleasant; he is kind to dumb animals, and to him children are a joy.

His health is not broken, his intelligence is not atrophied, he is still alert and brisk—in fact, he is too much so. He knows all there is to be known about prisons, and he knows the "ropes" too.

At liberty, he makes war upon society. In prison, he bows to the inevitable and makes the best of things. He is, and always has been, prepared to take the consequences, if caught, of his crime. But he has never yet persuaded himself, or tried to persuade himself, that he is a fool.

If again allowed liberty, he will cheerfully prepare for another campaign, and hope for a "long run." He weighs things up, for he is a logician, and so many crimes are equal to so much detention.

I have many of this man's letters from various prisons. I have details of his daily life. He tells of being in hospital and of his better food; he tells me that he is hoping for liberty and means to see me again. But he never makes any complaint, neither does he complain at liberty. Many hours have I spent with him discussing his life and prospects, crime and prison, but no complaint about his treatment has he ever uttered. Although habitually criminal, he considered himself much above the bulk of prisoners, and he will tell, ingenuously enough, that "prison is too good for most of them." Yet he had carried fire-arms and shot a policeman. He was not well educated, but he had read a great deal while in prison, where he had picked up a smattering of French.

He was a clever workman, and had developed a special branch

of his trade during his many detentions. As a prisoner he is perfect, as a citizen he is atrocious and impossible.

If we ask the half-mad fellow who is constantly in prison for deeds of violence to whom uncontrolled liberty means joy and life, we shall be able to read his answer in his eyes; they tell us that revenge is his great hope. But if we ask the aimless and hopeless wanderer who has been certified again and again as "unfit for prison discipline," we find no evidence of passion, no sense of grievance and no signs to indicate that prison was an undesirable place. Did not old "Cakebread" go cheerfully to prison, although her detentions numbered over three hundred!

If we seek an opinion from tramps and vagrants, they, if honest, will tell us that from time to time prison is a necessity to them; that if they cannot obtain entrance for vagrancy, why, then they will break somebody's window and so make sure of prison comforts, for it is "better than the workhouse."

If we consult youthful ex-prisoners, i.e. juvenile-adults, of whom unfortunately I know many, we get an altogether too favourable picture of prison life.

Many of them do not hesitate to tell us that they can "do it on their heads." Though physically this may be an exaggeration, yet the expression conveys a pretty accurate description of the effect imprisonment has had upon them. Lest it be thought that I am satisfied with prisons as they are at present, I will point out the reforms which I consider necessary in our penal system and our prison administration.

1. There is too much indiscriminate and unnecessary gaoling; prisons should be the last resource, not, as too frequently happens, the first.

In England and Wales alone nearly 100,000 persons are committed to prison every year because they cannot promptly pay fines that have been imposed for minor offences.

I hold that every offender fined, if she or he possesses a settled home, should be allowed adequate time to pay the fine. Probably this would keep 40,000 first offenders out of prison every year, with a corresponding reduction in the number of second offenders in the following years.

What folly can equal the plan of bundling a decent man or youth into the prison van, and putting all the machinery of prison into operation because he cannot pay forthwith a few shillings!

2. The old law of restitution and reparation must be revised. The First Offenders Act, now superseded by the Probation Act, was not an unmixed blessing, for, while it kept thousands of dishonest persons out of prison, it never convinced them of the serious nature of dishonesty. To use their own expression, "they were jolly well out of it"; consequently the wrong done to the individual was not impressed upon them. The law had been satisfied, to them nothing else mattered.

At the instigation of the Howard Association, Mr. Gladstone added a clause to the Probation Act empowering courts of summary jurisdiction to order restitution for goods or money stolen up to the value of £10. But magistrates do not put this clause in force; yet such a clause is not only just, but merciful.

Nothing can be worse for a young rogue than to know that he has stolen a considerable sum of money, and spent it in wicked waste without anything happening to him. Undoubtedly prison is bad for youths, for a month soon goes, but during that time character, aspiration and industry go also.

For the life of me I cannot see why orders for restitution should not be made; neither can I see any objection to our numerous probation officers having charge of these cases and collecting by instalments the money ordered.

For nothing will so effectually bring home to dishonest youths the enormity of the offences more than compulsion to pay back that which they have stolen.

Restitution would also be the greatest punishment for adult offenders in this direction.

For the forger, the burglar, the maker of counterfeit coins, the manufacturer of spurious notes, and all clever, calculating and persistent rogues other methods should be tried, for prison cannot demoralise them.

But for a first offender, even though he be of years, who has committed some breach of honesty, restitution seems the most effective way: the only reasonable plan for the prevention of demoralisation and the expense of prison.

Given, then, reasonable time for the payment of fines, a

thorough application of the Probation Act, and the establishment of compulsory but limited restitution—given these, half our prisons may be closed. Quite recently the governor of a large London prison declared that one-fourth of the daily average of his prisoners ought not to be in prison at all. I believe that statement to be below, not beyond the truth. We can easily see that if our prison population were reduced by one-half, great reforms would naturally follow in prison administration. Practically there would be the same amount of work to do in prison, for the various government departments would still require the commodities that prison labour supplies.

Prisons would then become hives of industry instead of castles of indolence, and prisoners would, of course, be given a much larger financial interest in the work done. Under such conditions, prisons, too, would naturally become pathological and psychological observatories. With proper men, and proper time to make the observations, prisons would reveal to us some of the dark wonders incident to the strange mixture of humanity we thoughtlessly dub criminal. When that happy day comes we shall be able to differentiate between crime and disease; we shall no longer punish men for their afflictions, but we shall treat them as patients in places other than prisons. Look for a moment at that growing, ever-growing army of people, the feeble-minded and irresponsibles—prisoners who are perpetually haled in prison, and to whose ranks four hundred are added every year. From prison to the streets, from the streets to the police station, from the station to the police court, and from thence to prison forms the vicious circle of their hopeless lives.

Certified as "unfit for prison discipline," yet everlastingly in prison; not fit for liberty, yet constantly thrust into liberty; homeless, hopeless, friendless, battered from pillar to post, eyesores to humanity, they tread the vicious circle. Some day we shall pity them and care for them and give them, under control, as much childlike happiness as they can appreciate—such work as they can do with simple comforts and controlling discipline; but no useless liberty, no opportunities of perpetuating their kind, no more of the vicious circle and no more prison. And the tramps and the loafers, too, must be taken in hand, and not with a gloved hand either, for prison is no place for them. The month or six weeks is soon over. They have been cleansed, they have recuperated. Then, heigho! for the hedgerows if it is summer, the Embankment or shelters if it is winter.

Their vagrant days must end, and end in detention in some place where the wholesome Pauline advice may be carried out—if they will not work, neither shall they eat! but with no chance of a second generation. And there is another class of whom I must speak, but I do so with fear and trembling: I refer to the wild and gross women who live upon our streets, and whose individual convictions number anything between twenty and four hundred. Look! during the year 1906, 933 women, each of whom had served more than ten imprisonments, were once more in Holloway Gaol.

Some hundreds of them had been in that gaol more than twenty times each! Many of them were known personally to me; for I had seen them in the cells, and I had seen them at liberty; I had seen them drunk, and I had seen them sober.

But whether sober or drunk, they are slaves of a gross, overmastering passion elemental in its intensity—to them nothing else matters.

But the State says they are inebriates, and treats them as such. Yet drink is but an incident in their lives and effect, and the cause of their condition lies deeper, much deeper. Down through generations some germs have come and have found an abiding-place in their bodies, bearing fruition in their terrible and hopeless lives. Is an ordinary prison a place for them? is one month's, two months' or six months' detention of any avail in their case? I think not!

But ask the prison authorities, or consult the records, and you will get an answer! Do the claims of humanity ask for no consideration? has science nothing to say upon the matter? Are we to go on for ever tinkering with a vital question, giving such women an endless succession of short imprisonments which only serve the purpose of renewing their health that their lives may be devoted to the most fearful purpose to which any human being can be subjected?

But when all these unfortunate classes are properly cared for, we shall still require prisons; but they must be specialised prisons, and our officials must be properly qualified and equipped for their work.

The science of healing must play a more important part; the doctor must be a student of mental as well as physical diseases.

When the days of short imprisonments are ended we shall

probably have a "receiving prison" to which the offenders will be sent on conviction for "observation" and "classification," and thence drafted to different prisons suitable to their age, condition and ability. For a plan of this description would bring the duties of governors, doctors, chaplains and warders, within the sphere of possibility. Failing this, strive as they may and do, we ask them to perform the impossible. But in the prisons of the future, specialised as they will be, classification will still have to play an important part; but classification will be no longer governed by the number of convictions a youth or adult has received but by the real character, temperament and ability of the prisoner.

And in these prisons there will be work demanding the use of muscle or fingers; there will be opportunities for the use of brains, and some chance for the emotions of the heart to have play.

Consider for a moment the life of a man undergoing a five years' sentence. It is one of deadening routine! With mechanical certitude his actions are controlled and ordered: the same food in amount and kind at the same time each day and served in the same manner.

The same amount of cell, the same amount of bed, no opportunities of doing kindnesses, no opportunities for receiving kindnesses, his brain, heart and muscles alike are kept stagnant. Yet he schools himself to deceive, for he knows that if he plays the hypocrite long enough he will reduce his sentence by fifteen months. Consequently he develops a servile manner and a low cunning. Let any otherwise decent man live this life for three years and nine months, always having before him the one object—that of shortening his term—and I need not ask what the psychological result will be.

Yes! this bribe to good behaviour must be abolished, even though Captain Maconachie arise from his grave to defend it. And the prisons of the future will know it not, for the prisoner's release will be determined by other conditions than mere mechanical obedience. And with the passing of the "ticket-of-leave," "police supervision" is also passing; truly it is time that both were dead and buried. Perhaps I may astonish some folk by stating that "police supervision," notwithstanding its impressive sound, was a farce absolute and complete.

An ex-convict had no fear of it. He could "report" himself by letter! and I have never, though I have often inquired into such complaints, found the statements about detective and police interference with the employment of discharged prisoners justified; neither have I known any "old lag" who found the supervision irksome in the least degree.

The conditions were too easily fulfilled; an occasional visit to the police station, and then reporting by letter sufficed. But sometimes we are apt to forget that even employers and the public have a right to consideration equally with the discharged prisoners. Supposing, as not infrequently happens, a dangerous rogue obtains a situation of trust by the aid of forged character and references. What can the police do? What ought they to do if honest? but I am quite certain any officer that needlessly interfered with an ex-convict who was honestly trying to obtain a livelihood would get scant mercy from his superiors. The police and detective force know this quite well.

Mr. Gladstone's Preventive Detention Act will do much to lighten the labour of Scotland Yard. The pity is that it limits a sentence of preventive detention to ten years; for at the expiration of this time, whatever be the age, mental and physical condition or past record of the prisoner sentenced under the Act, he must be discharged though he be homeless, hopeless and friendless. He may, of course, be discharged much earlier if circumstances warrant, especially if he has friends and work to take up.

Now the men who qualify for the provisions of this Act are of two classes. First: the determined and persistent criminal who lives by crime, desires to live by crime, and to whom no other life has any attraction.

Against these men, after being adjudged by a jury to be habitual criminals, we ought to be safeguarded even as we protect ourselves against known madmen.

The second class are criminals because they are quite irresponsible—a helpless class of individuals who have not the ability to maintain themselves, who can do nothing useful unless under control. Most of the men who comprise these two classes are of middle age, many of them decidedly old. When their preventive detention expires they will be ten years older. I question the mercy, as well as the justice of thrusting these old men into useless liberty. Surely it would be better to detain them under reasonable conditions, to let them quietly die out in the hope that few will be found to take their places. And in the days to come that most woefully afflicted human, the epileptic, will not wear the criminal badge or the convict's brand, and the hideous cruelty inflicted on these unfortunates will be no longer perpetrated.

Their sorrows and their sufferings will make no vain appeal to our pity and care, for we shall protect them and ourselves in a human and scientific way; but not in prison! And when that time comes the horrid term "criminal lunatic" will also disappear from our vocabulary, for it is high time this classification was buried and numbered with the monstrosities of the past.

I protest against this phrase and the consequences that attach to it. Verily it passes the wit of men to conceive how any one can be a criminal and a lunatic at one and the same time, for if he be the one he cannot be the other. So Broadmoor will become the "State Asylum," and the cruel farce of putting undeniably insane people on their trial will no longer be tolerated, for quietly and mercifully, after due certification they will pass to the mental hospital with no brand of criminality upon them. But I would ask: Are we to be for ever impotent before disease of the brain? Are physical afflictions and deprivations to remain for ever unconsidered when justice holds the scales, and when punishment is decreed? I think not! nay, I am sure, for in the prisons that are yet to be the paternal hand of the State, while exercising a restraining power over its stricken children, will consider their afflictions and limitations and have mercy upon them.

Then, blighted youth, blighted through poverty; disease, malformation or accident will be no longer neglected even though it be criminally inclined; then, the reproach that the State helps only those that can help themselves will be wiped out; then, even in our prisons, the weaklings will receive some portion of their due, and the days of criminal neglect will be ended.

THE END